The Nature Kid's Guide to
SEAHORSES

DAVID ANDERSON

LP Media Inc. Publishing
Text copyright © 2026 by LP Media Inc.
All rights reserved.

For information address LP Media Inc. Publishing,
30012 Variolite St NW, Princeton MN 55371
www.lpmedia.org

Publication Data

Seahorses
The Nature Kid's Guide to Seahorses — First edition.

Summary: "Learn all about Seahorses, the Nature Kid Way"
— Provided by publisher.

ISBN: 979-8-89818-235-9

[1. Seahorses – Non-Fiction] I. Title.

Title: The Nature Kid's Guide to Seahorses

CONTENTS

FISHY SURPRISE

Swish! A tiny seahorse floats upright through the sea.

Seahorses are fish — but you would never guess it by looking at them. Instead of scales they wear bony armor, and instead of swimming flat like other fish, they bob upright through the water like tiny horses trotting through the waves. That is exactly how they got their name.

Like all fish, seahorses breathe through **gills** and steer with small fins on their back and head. But almost nothing else about them follows the rules.

A seahorse has no teeth and no stomach. Food passes straight through its body in minutes, which means it has to eat almost constantly just to survive.

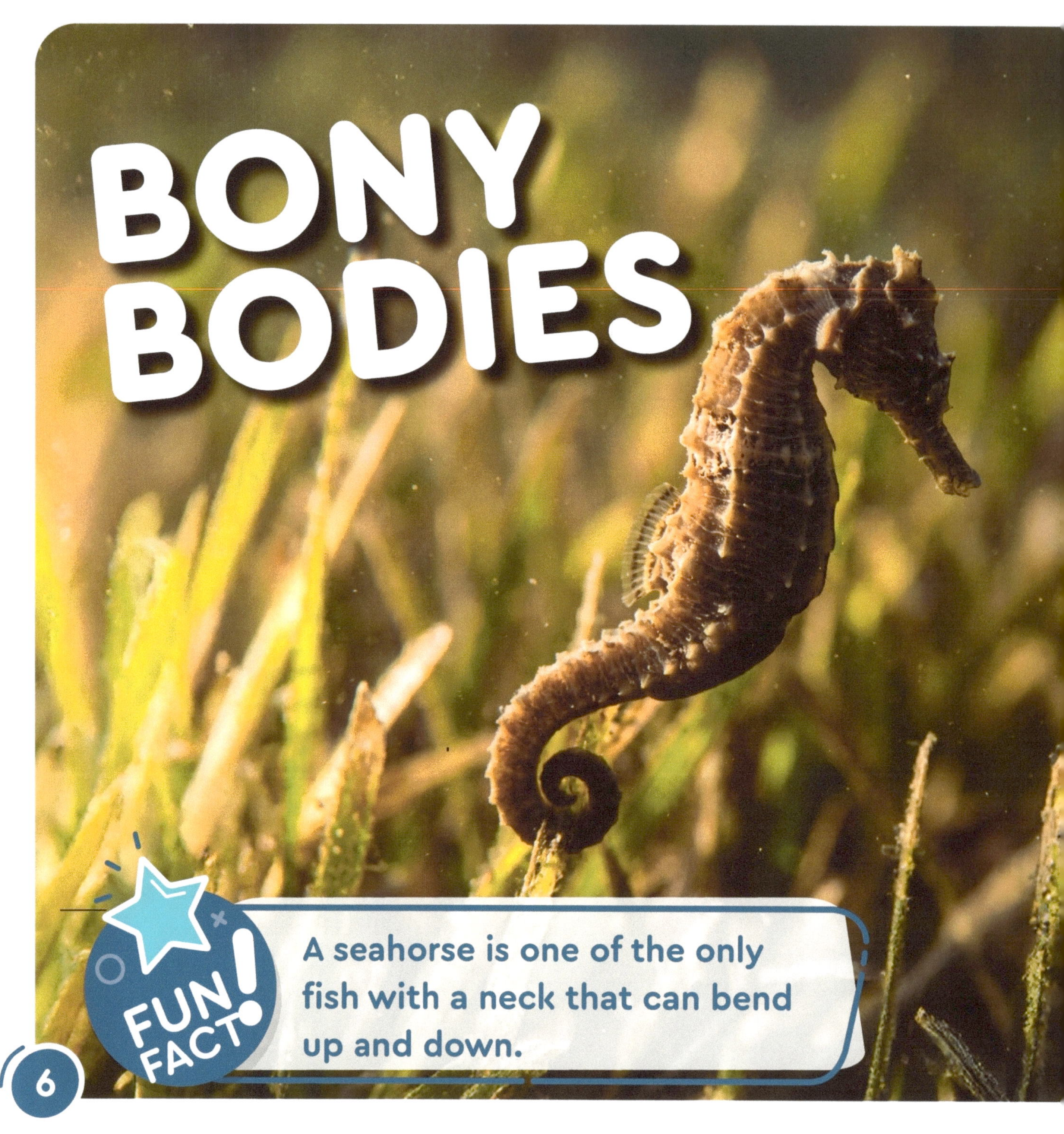

BONY BODIES

A seahorse is one of the only fish with a neck that can bend up and down.

Clink! Hard bony plates lock together like tiny armor.

Most fish have smooth scales. Seahorses do not. They have bony rings around their body, and these rings act like a suit of armor. About 50 rings protect a single seahorse!

A seahorse has a long, curly tail. It wraps its tail around seagrass or coral to hold on tight. This keeps it safe in strong currents.

On its head sits a small bump called a **coronet**. Every seahorse has a different one. It is like a fingerprint, unique to each fish!

SUPER DADS

A seahorse dad can give birth to over 1,000 babies at one time!

Pop! Pop! Pop! Tiny babies shoot out of their dad's pouch.

Seahorse dads do something amazing. They carry the babies! The mom puts her eggs into a **pouch** on the dad's belly, and he keeps them safe and warm.

The eggs grow for two to four weeks. Then the dad squeezes his body back and forth. Tiny babies pop out one by one!

Baby seahorses are very small, no bigger than a grain of rice. They float away right after birth and must find food and hide from **predators** all by themselves.

SNEAKY STRIKERS

Snap! A seahorse sucks up a tiny shrimp faster than you can blink.

Seahorses are the slowest fish in the sea. The dwarf seahorse swims only five feet per hour. That is slower than most snails!

But seahorses have a secret weapon. Their long snout can strike in just one millisecond. That is faster than the blink of an eye! Water and food get sucked right in.

Seahorses wait very still near the grass. When tiny shrimp swim by, they strike fast. The shrimp never see it coming.

DEVOTED DANCERS

When seahorses first meet, they may dance for up to eight hours straight!

12

Splish! Two seahorses spin and twirl in a morning dance.

Many seahorses pick one partner for life. Each morning, they greet each other with a dance. They swim side by side and change colors together.

The pair links tails and spins around. Their dance can last for many minutes. It helps them stay close and recognize each other in the crowded sea.

If one partner is lost, the other may wait a long time. Some seahorses look for a new mate. Others keep waiting and waiting, sometimes for weeks.

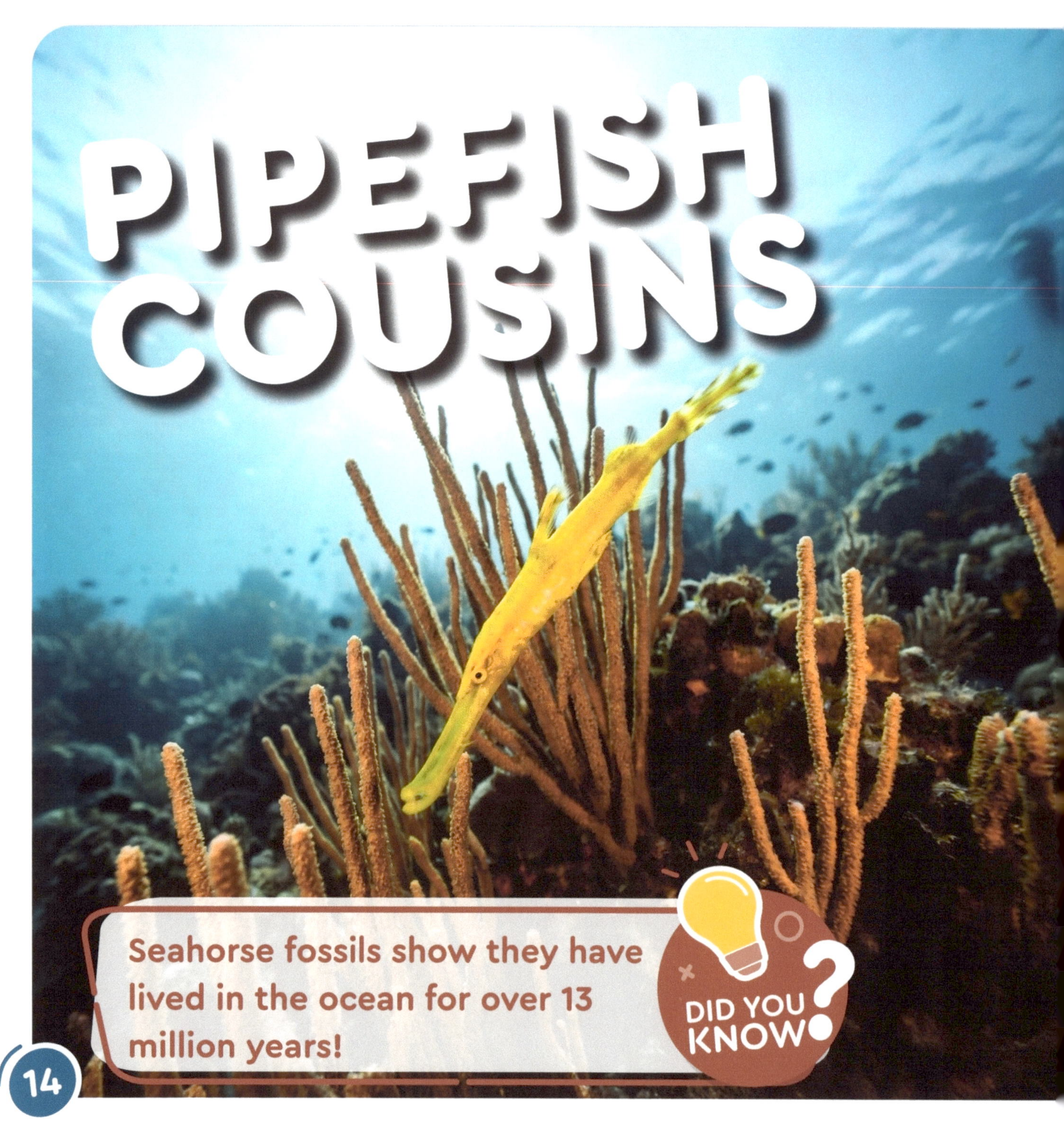

PIPEFISH COUSINS

Whoosh! A long, thin pipefish darts through the coral reef.

Seahorses belong to a big family called **Syngnathidae** (sin-NATH-ih-dee). That is a long word! It means 'fused jaw.' All the fish in this group have long snouts shaped like tubes.

Pipefish and sea dragons are in this family too. Pipefish look like thin sticks. Sea dragons look like bits of floating seaweed. There are over 300 species in all!

All of these fish share one cool thing. The dads care for the young, not the moms. In this family, fathers do most of the work!

COMMON SEAHORSES

Psst! A spotted seahorse hides among the swaying seagrass.

One seahorse has a short little snout. People call it the common seahorse. But it is not easy to find at all! It is actually quite rare.

This seahorse lives in shallow water near Europe. It hides in seagrass beds and can be brown, yellow, green, or even purple. Each one looks a little different.

So why call a rare fish 'common?' Scientists named it long ago, before they knew how hard it was to find. The name just stuck!

TINY TRICKSTERS

Some pygmy seahorses spend their whole life on one single piece of coral and never leave.

Shh! A seahorse smaller than your fingernail hides on coral.

Pygmy seahorses are some of the tiniest fish in the sea. Most are smaller than a grape! They live on soft coral fans in warm ocean water.

These tiny seahorses are masters of hiding. Their bumpy skin matches the coral they live on perfectly. Even expert divers have a hard time seeing them.

Scientists did not find the first one on purpose. Someone was studying coral in a lab when a tiny seahorse crawled out! What a surprise that must have been!

BIG BELLIES

A big-bellied seahorse can live in water that is over 100 feet deep!

Splash! A big seahorse puffs out its round belly and swims.

The big-bellied seahorse is one of the largest in the world. It can grow up to 14 inches long. That is about as tall as a ruler!

This seahorse lives in the waters around Australia and New Zealand. It hangs out in bays and shallow reefs, where its round belly gives it its fun name.

Big-bellied seahorses come in many colors. Some are yellow. Others are brown, cream, or white. Many have dark spots scattered all over their bodies.

STRIPED SWIMMERS

Gurgle! A zebra seahorse bobs near a bright coral reef.

The zebra seahorse has bold white stripes on a dark body. It looks a lot like a tiny zebra! This rare seahorse is found only near northern Australia.

Zebra seahorses live around coral reefs in warm, clear water. They stay close to sponges and rocks for shelter. They are shy and do not move far from home.

Not much is known about zebra seahorses yet. They are hard to find and study. Scientists hope to learn more about how they live and what they eat.

SHARP SPINES

24

Prick! Sharp spines stick out all over this tough seahorse.

The thorny seahorse is covered in long, sharp spines. These spines help scare away predators. Would you want to bite something that pointy? Most fish swim right past!

Thorny seahorses live in warm ocean waters across the Pacific and Indian Oceans. They hide among seagrass, rocks, and soft coral.

These seahorses can grow to about seven inches long. Their spiny look helps them blend in with the bumpy reef around them. They are true survivors of the sea!

LEAFY LEGENDS

DID YOU KNOW?

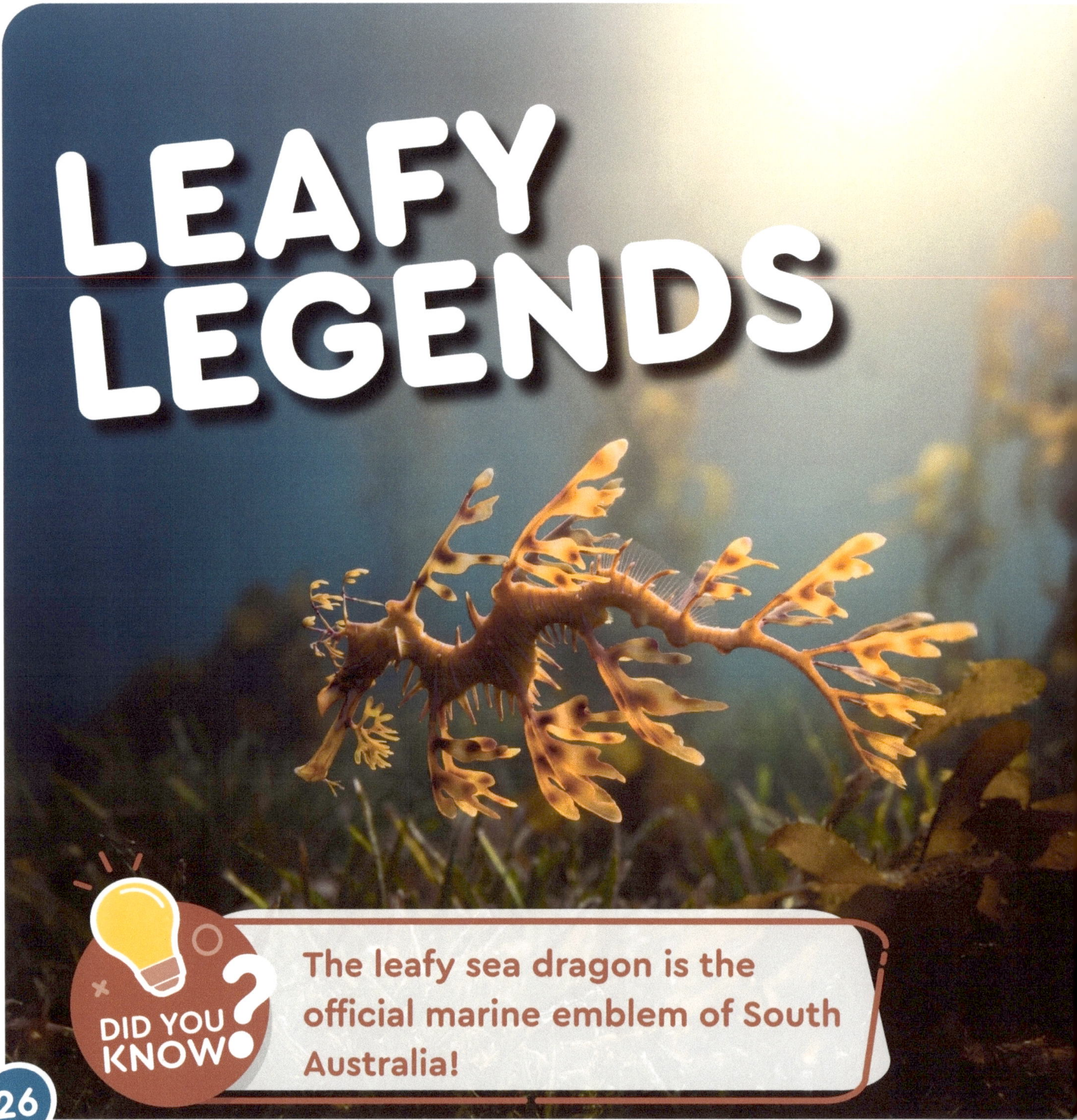

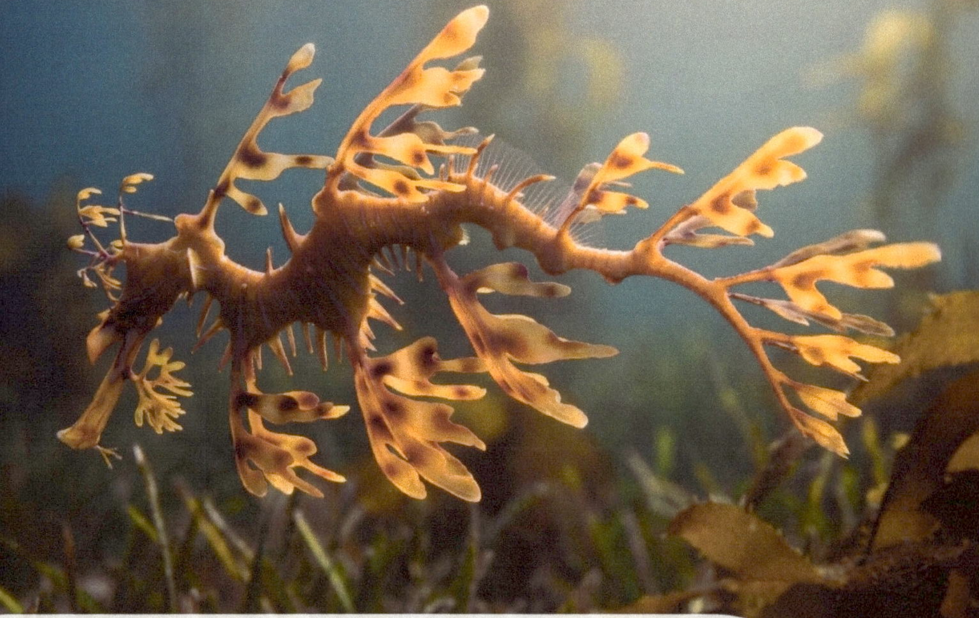

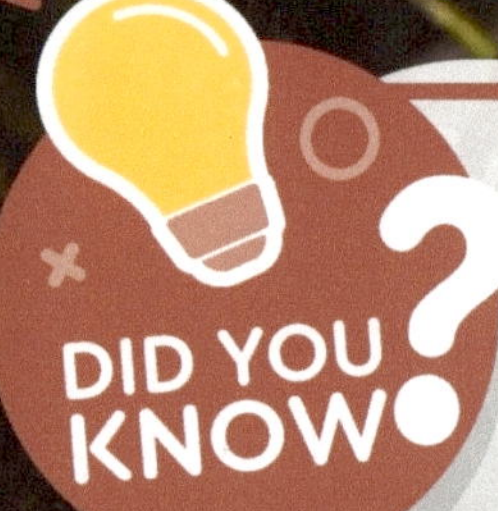

The leafy sea dragon is the official marine emblem of South Australia!

Swoosh! A creature that looks like floating seaweed glides by.

The leafy sea dragon is the fanciest fish in the sea. Long, leafy flaps cover its body from head to tail. It looks just like a piece of floating seaweed!

Leafy sea dragons live off the south coast of Australia. They drift through kelp and seagrass beds, and their leafy skin keeps them safe from predators who swim right past.

Unlike seahorses, these sea dragons cannot grip with their tails. They just float along with the waves. They are gentle, slow, and very hard to spot.

WEEDY WONDERS

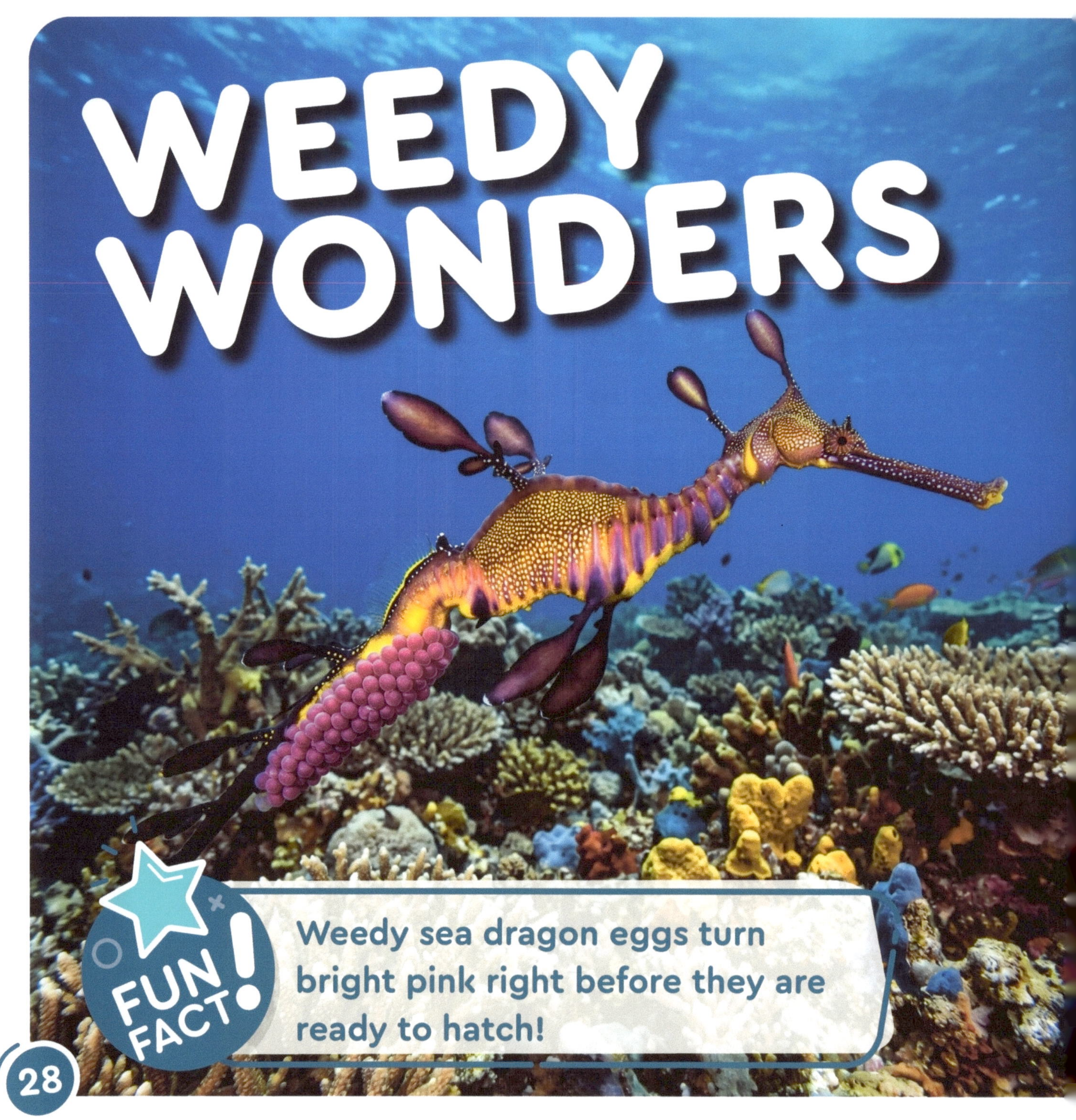

28

Rustle! A weedy sea dragon sways back and forth in the current.

The weedy sea dragon is a cousin of the leafy one. But it looks a bit different. It has smaller flaps that look like floating weeds instead of big leaves.

Weedy sea dragons live in southern and eastern Australia. They swim near rocky reefs and sandy patches close to shore, growing up to 18 inches long.

The dad carries the eggs under his tail. He has no pouch like a seahorse. Instead, the eggs stick right to his skin until they hatch about eight weeks later.

RUBY REVEALED

Scientists used an underwater robot to film the first living ruby sea dragon!

Blub! A bright red sea dragon swims in the deep, dark sea.

The ruby sea dragon is the newest in its family. Scientists named it in 2015. No one had seen a living one until 2016!

This sea dragon is deep red with pink stripes. It lives in deep water off western Australia, much deeper than its leafy and weedy cousins. Some live 160 feet below the surface!

The ruby sea dragon has no leafy flaps at all. Its smooth body helps it glide through the deep sea. There is still so much to learn about this mysterious fish.

PIPEFISH PUZZLES

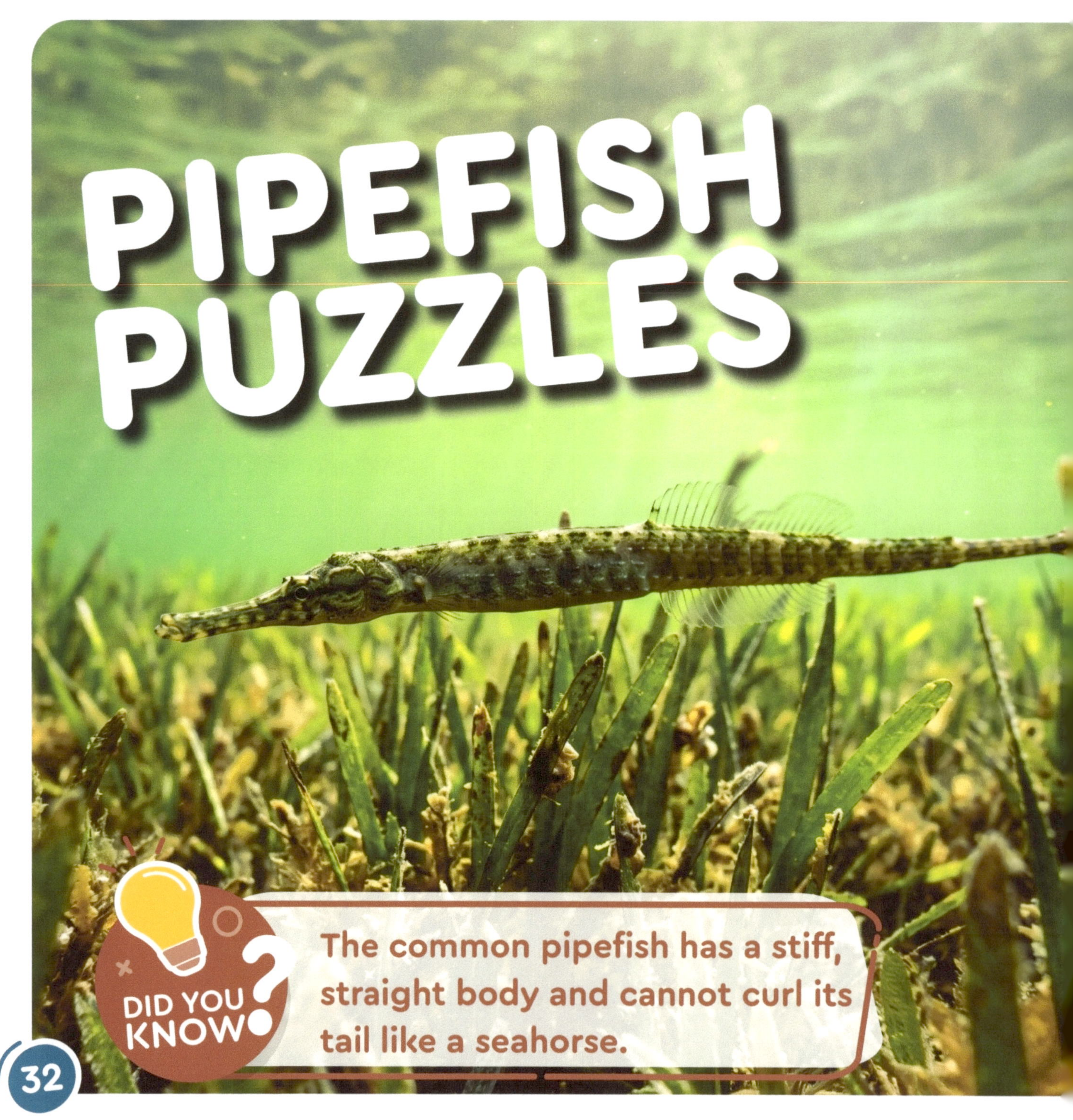

Zip! A long, thin pipefish zips through the seagrass like a needle.

Pipefish are close cousins of seahorses. They are long and thin, like little pipes. That is how they got their name!

The common pipefish lives in shallow water near Europe. It hides in beds of seagrass and sea plants, where its slim shape makes it very hard to see. Some grow up to 18 inches long!

Pipefish dads carry the eggs too. The eggs rest in a groove under the dad's belly, and he keeps them safe until they hatch. Fatherhood runs in the family!

CLICKING CAMO

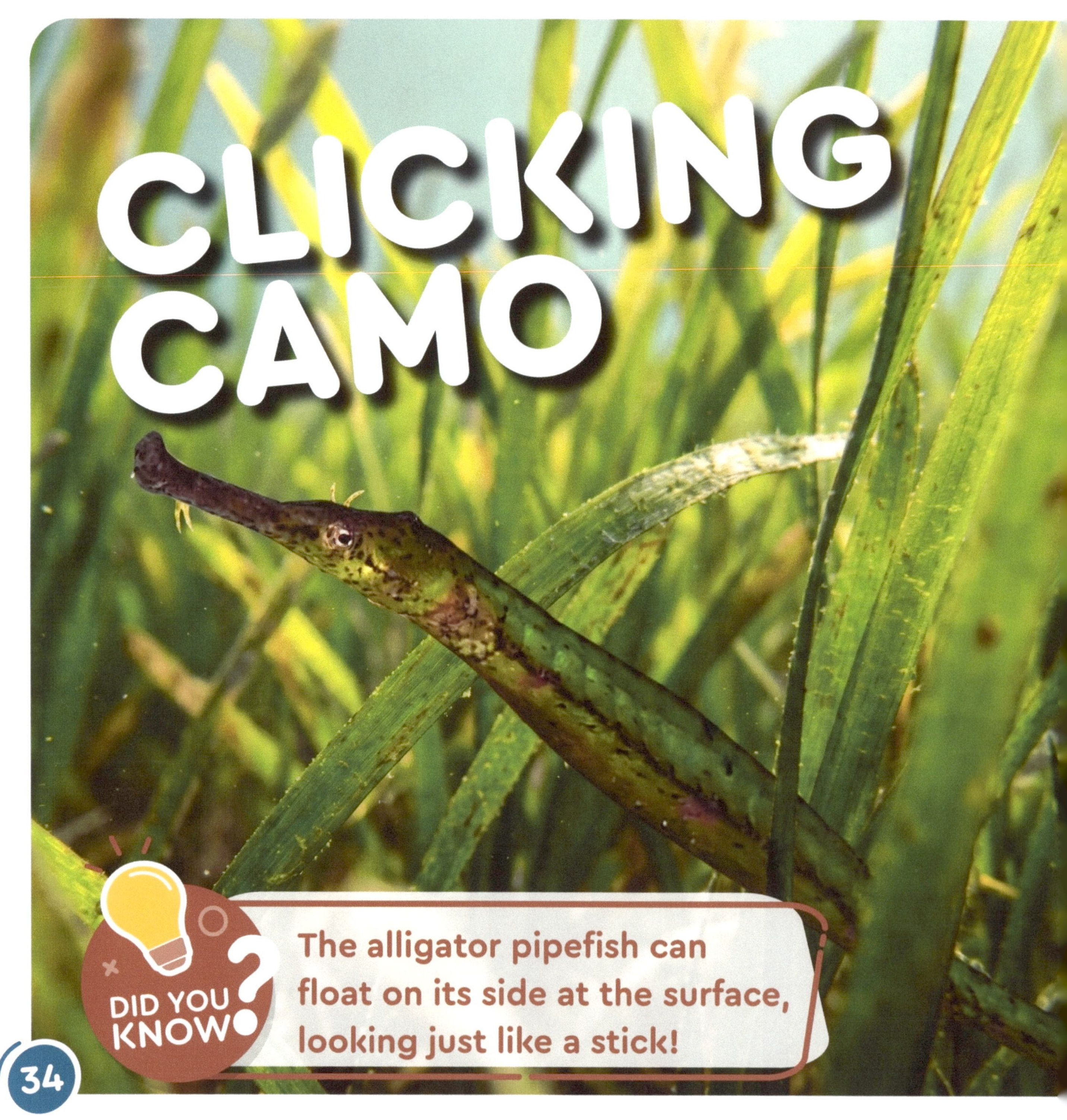

The alligator pipefish can float on its side at the surface, looking just like a stick!

Click, click! A big pipefish makes sounds like snapping fingers.

The alligator pipefish is the biggest pipefish in the world. It can grow to about a foot long! Its bumpy snout looks a bit like an alligator's nose.

This pipefish lives in warm waters across Asia and Australia. It hides in seagrass and near mangrove roots, where its green and brown colors help it stay hidden.

Alligator pipefish can make clicking sounds. Scientists think they click to talk to each other. How cool is a fish that clicks like snapping fingers!

SEAHORSE SURVIVAL

Some aquariums raise baby seahorses and release them into the sea to help wild populations grow!

Scrape! The ocean floor gets torn up as a fishing net drags across it.

Seahorses are in trouble. Every year, millions are taken from the sea. Some are sold as medicine. Others are dried and sold in shops as souvenirs.

Dirty water hurts seahorses too. When seagrass beds are ripped up, seahorses lose their homes. Warmer oceans make life even harder for them.

But people are working to help! Some countries now protect seahorses by law. Scientists are looking for new ways to keep their ocean homes safe. You can help by keeping beaches clean!

FORGOTTEN FISH

A group of seahorses is sometimes called a herd, just like horses on land!

Flutter! A seahorse bobs past, waving its tiny fin like a little flag.

Seahorses may be small, but they are full of wonder. They hide, they dance, and they surprise us at every turn. Scientists are still learning new things about them every year.

You now know more about seahorses than most people! You know about their family, their homes, and the dangers they face. That makes you a seahorse expert.

The ocean needs our help. When we keep the sea clean and safe, we help seahorses too. Tell a friend what you learned today!

GLOSSARY

gills
Body parts that help fish breathe in water

coronet
The small bump on top of a seahorse's head

predator
An animal that hunts and eats other animals

Syngnathidae
The family of fish that includes seahorses and pipefish

pouch
A pocket of skin where a seahorse dad holds eggs